Lyricism and the Electric

Published in the United States of America by SPACE

Design by: Maritta Tapanainen
Editor: Russell Leong

S P ▲ C E
2044 Mayview Drive
Los Angeles, California 90027

Cover: *Patrecia, in Egypt*
Michael J. Laurence
Collage, 1994

LIBRARY OF CONGRESS CATALOG CARD NUMBER 96-67851
ISBN 0-9649233-0-0 (Softcover)

Night Owl

Owl wings by mottled moonlight.
We see the beauty
of suddenly spread wings,
hear their delineating of space.

"American Beauty"

On an assemblage by Bruce Brodie

We do not see the small prey,
only hear its terror,
last sounds rising
~~*beneath elegantly gliding wings.*~~
beneath wings riding upward.

She circles around and around
behind a semi-transparent screen,
colored lights behind her.

That familiar form
recognizable
and precise

colored lights behind her,
~~*constant*~~ ~~*behind by a screen*~~
~~*of semi-transparency.*~~

obscured by an almost
opaque screen.

only when she nears the screen,
enticing shadows otherwise,
mysterious,
elusive outlines;
artful voyeurism of art.

That This beauty is a tiny airplane
circling within a box frame
makes making it a symbol
of a symbol:
that cute phenomenon
of why men name
their war planes
using women's names.

But this beauty
is a tiny airplane,
a boy's own toy,
phallus with wings
circling within a box frame.

Symbol of a symbol:
that cute phenomena
of why men name
their war planes
~~*using women's names.*~~

Poor 'American Beauty'
trapped in her
endless circle,
~~*a borrowed name*~~
~~helpless symbol.~~
~~this sexual toy~~
~~helpless symbol.~~

labeled with
a borrowed name,
helpless symbol.

Lyricism and the Electric

Poems by
Michael J. Laurence

Preface by Josine Ianco-Starrels

S P A C E • Los Angeles • California • 1996

Preface

I THINK OF LIFE AND DEATH QUITE FREQUENTLY THESE DAYS—
of sunlight turning dark and darkness turning grey.
Fair hair turns grey gently—without dramatic transitions.
It fades slowly, imperceptibly, into delicately ashen hues like
an erased drawing. When last I saw Michael his engaging
smile still illuminated that boyishly handsome face but weary
eyes betrayed sadness and his hair was turning gently grey.

I knew him for years and yet I knew him not; I had always
marvelled at his charming presence and at the clarity of his
thoughts, yet I learned more about him through the poems I
read after he was gone. His elegantly placid exterior disguised
a complicated, seething soul. Chronicler and raconteur,
urbane and articulate, he always injected that dash of humor
which makes life bearable.

Although reserved—almost self-effacing—he was an astute
observer carefully assessing intentions, savoring insights,
distilling impressions. Later, when the noises of the day
subsided, these were meticulously processed and transformed
into words. His critical writing was never sharp or cutting—
he said what he had to say with grace and eloquence.

In his personal work, Michael assembled bouquets of
forgotten objects, vestiges of events, sensations, memories,
and visions molding them into visual and verbal poems. He

rearranged experience—pressed life between the pages of his own sensibility, like flowers gathered on a walk in the woods.

Sometimes I think that each of us is allotted a given number of days on this earth, each day, one page in the stack constituting a lifetime. As time passes, the stack diminishes—the number of pages apportioned to each of us is a secret no one has yet uncovered. What remains after we're gone is the work we have done, the friends we have made, the people we have loved and who loved us—the way we behaved while we were on this earth.

Michael will always be part of us—those of us who had the privilege of knowing him, even if we knew but a small part of him. He lived well. Michael did not waste time on inconsequential matters. He listened, he travelled, he looked and really saw what he was looking at. He understood without becoming arrogant and was sensitive to feelings without getting lost in sentimentality. Toward the end he faced truth without self-delusion, which takes great courage. He was passionate, wise, tender and vulnerable—as all true poets are.

Josine Ianco-Starrels

Lyricism and the Electric

Contents

Lyricism and the Electric

Owl wings by mottled moonlight.
        We see the thrill
                of suddenly spread wings,
hear their definitions of space.

We cannot see the small prey,
        only hear its sound
                last cries rising
beneath wings riding upward.

Everything has its place in nature
        which we cannot condemn:
                lyricism and the electric
joined in a terrifying plan.

Two Views of Paradise

I. Born with beauty not common sense
     the chain restaurant hostess
  was a once-famous New York model.
End of day and sudden Miami rain
    glazes her licorice black hair.
Her face, thin as a gazelle's,
    is lined under its mask
    of dead-white make-up.

What she once possessed is gone,
    like mercury running
loosely through her fingers.

      She arrives at her motel.
Blank television screen,
single, narrow bed,
    swimming pool's flat surface
    surrounded by dying palm trees.

The green neon sign signals
     this place is 'Paradise.'

II. His grime encrusted hands repeat
    decades of repeated motions.
      He guides his felucca past
a palm tree oasis along the Nile.
      He is not thinking
of home or of his children's children.
    Images rise fresh as yesterday:
    a brief affair in Cairo;
    time, late 1940's.

Slide of naked flesh against
    bare flesh, their bodies
    crossing class lines
      on green cotton sheets
soft and thin with constant washing

Wind rising moves the felucca
    smoothly across green water.

Parallel Objects

Form following
the other's function.
Similar differences.
Starfish and sand dollar.
Plate and imprint
like a door
both exit and entrance
or a stairway

A boat is
best steered
with two oars.
Nature gives
example:
what can fly
with only one wing?

Photograph of a Floss Silk Tree in Bloom

How oddly calm
    this peculiar scene
unreal/hyper-real
    freshness of nightmare
    in ordinary reality

the nearly naked man
    straddling
    unwillingly
    ungainly
the upright trunk
of the floss silk tree

with its row
    upon row
        upon row
of short
    sharp
        thorns

ropes from wrist to wrist
ankle to ankle
    medieval torture
    updated to modern sport

punctured
partially supported
on sharp thorns
    any movement
    muscle twitch
    involuntary
    self-inflicted punishment

graceless prisoner
attended by three soldiers
    casually at-ease
    two with stupid eyes
    one with a nervous expression
waiting for guilt admission
or information
or merely slow death

sadism as
politic's servant

torture methods
in dark rooms
    naked lightbulbs
    black hoods
    electrical circuits
all too familiar

brought out
into daylight
    into nature
    using nature
using outdoor exhibition
as public example

sturdy back
lash marked
head lolling
    broken eyeglasses
    hanging askew

dark red blood
channeling down
pale green tree bark
    marking expired time
    coagulating in pools
    on hard ground

someone must have
taken this photograph

possibly another soldier
perhaps as souvenir
or other grotesque reason
    this record of nothing new
    except man's inhumanity

a photograph records
without discrimination

including
    floss silk blossoms
    on the ground
which are pink and white
like orchids

October 29, 1988

Fog over the moon tonight
yet the evening star is sharp in higher air.
White chrysanthemums
like muted lights
edge the garden
chilled with autumn.
Darkness deepens.

Knots, Coming Untied

Frequencies crackling with static
with messages to the unwary,
crisp as fresh news.
Like an abruptly clear view
from a descending helicopter.
If daily occurrences
wore silk kimonos and spoke
metaphysically and in Armenian,
would they pay it more attention?
One learns to live if uneasily
on the lips of an earthquake
providing its mouth is closed.
Armfuls of wet peonies
are always a better present
than boxes of broken glass.
Tune in your radio stations
carefully: that oboe and cello
concerto will be interrupted:
weather reports predicting
the acid failure of love or
slowly falling, unforgivable
torrents of someone else's
undisciplined desire,
your territory taken by terrorists,
Nightmares at noon glued together
from fragments of disturbed childhoods.
Which fades faster: language or love?
Unpredictable endings echo
predictable beginnings.
No news from your enemies
is good news but of ostrich value.

Apropos of Empty Spaces

I

The bridge of early friendship
cannot cross the fatal widening distance.

II

After a night of torture, a political prisoner
faces an inevitably ordinary morning.

III

Tarnishing circles of my two wedding bands
rediscovered on another moving day.

IV

After a war, the flat pause in ruins
which once were cities.

V

Photographs of childhood show faces
we do not recognize but belonged to us.

VI

Falling back into clock time, lovers
slackly embrace intimate strangers.

VII

A widow's mirror, turned to the wall,
reflects nothing back but the wall.

VIII

Music, ending, amplifies silence.

Dreams and Cup Readings

for Violet Marriott

I.

Being one with the ignorant.
moving along with appearances.
Images in dreams and patterns in cups
strip sight to the bone.
It is a naked vision.
a perfect blindness to see
    stone in a stone
        straw in a straw
           reality in a dream

Exact images, images of other images.
Exact patterns, patterns of other patterns:
images in patterns, even patterns in images:

all mirror in the mind.
speechless voice echoing
from the other world.
Coming back on the curve of the universe.

II.

What do the cups tell?
The grounds form two sides in mine:
one contorted bodies.
emotional, alive with motion:
the other straight rows of marble columns.
monks and silence

The cup is scryed. In Greek
I am told of orgies in my youth.
A monastery in the future.
The former true. I live the future:
a plain bed in a narrow room.
Waking to reality in a dream
of waking reality.

There are two sides to every answer.

III.

Crossing the Straits of Gibraltar by ferry.
Spain disappears: distinct land, grey shape,
then only horizon. Morocco comes into view:
first horizon, grey shape, then distinct land.
The same, exactly opposite, the other way.
Doing push-ups on a mirror
is the same:
the world we touch, that other world.
They are the same.

Last year in Cuenca, Vi,
waiting for a late arriving Spanish train
you insisted did not exist
until it came clanging into view,
we talked about that other world
which is but is not,
of attaining perfect center
in the sacred zone.

Complicated duplications
requiring perfect attention
like a monk turning somersaults on a needle's point.

IV.

The young boy with melted wings
falls toward the water
while his image rises to the surface.

It is the same, exactly opposite, the other way.

V.

Your last letter from London
tells of being caught in the curve
climbing Glastonbury Tor,
its top a ruined church to St. Michael.

> *Stuck in a grove, I kept going round*
> *and round. As fast as I went up,*
> *sooner or later, returning to the same*
> *place. I tried to come down.*
> *At the bottom, searching for a gap*
> *in the thorn hedges, I found myself*
> *again slowly going up the spiral.*

We act the acrobat,
mimic the major in a minor mode,
find the exit is the entrance
and the entrance always exit.
Duplicated action in our dreams
is action duplicated from our waking;
the cup patterns images
from images already dreamed.

VI.

Where I live now,
this old Venetian ruin
set in a Cretan landscape
of pine, olive and palm
I dream of ancient orgies
and wake to a narrow room
to a dream of demanding sirens
singing to innocent seamen
and dreams of an empty room.

What was told as legend,
I live as plain fact,
yet what I live is more than myth:
here the priestess and the thread,
the young man and the dying bull
and those acrobat bull dancers
leaping in a mirror maze.

Somersaulting at the center
we become
    that stone in a stone
        that straw in a straw
            that reality in a dream
in the perfect naked vision
in the sacred zone
of absolute reality.

One Angel Street
Chania, Crete

III

Big Hot City Blues

"Are you having those Big Hot City Blues?"
Hart Crane, in a letter, 1930

As a matter of fact, I am
and it's fifty years later.
A different city but the heat
settles down like a slow
tarantula and I stall
like an overheated car
boiling over on the freeway.
Small respite in the early morning hours
but the hot fur of descending heat
presses down by afternoon,
the night sweating slide
of frictionless bodies
tangled in the soaking sheets
and alone again in the dust dry dawn,
incoherent ravings of nightmares
lingering among the damp towels.
Palm trees rattling
in the Santa Anas blowing hot
breath from the sandy desert,
yuccas stabbing like knives
from the seared hills here,
the streets below a heated grid iron.
Words clogged with sand and limp
poetry is not the concern
of sailors on shore leave with their
tight whites wilted and slightly soiled
or tired prostitutes along Sunset Boulevard
doing it for a cut rate in a parking lot
in the late night heat of 3 a.m.
The city renders us down like hot fat
writer sailor whore
cooked together in the big hot city.

A Wedding in Morocco

1. She stands out,
   half against the door,
   half against the wall.
Nearer
in the foreground
   an older woman
   with a great deal
   of white about her,
   which almost entirely
   conceals her.
Shadows
   full of reflections;
   white in the shadows.

2. A pillar stands out
   dark against
   the foreground.
The women on the left
rise in tiers
   one above the other
   like pots of flowers.
Gold and white
predominate;
   yellow handkerchiefs.
Children
   sitting on the ground
   in front.

3. The ceremony
through the day
   music, food,
   caravans of gifts.
The bride and groom
stand together
   but apart
   like strangers.

4. In the evening:
    the cries of the old women.
The young married woman
    painting her face,
    holding the candle
    while she is
    being dressed
The veil
    thrown over
    her face.
Girls standing on the bed.

5. He arrives
    with his attendants.
Everyone withdraws
to outer rooms
    Candles,
    shadows,
    rose petals,
    silence.
At sunrise,
    dogs bark
    in the courtyard.

6. During the day:
    the newly married women
    against the wall,
    their nearest relation
    acting as chaperons.
The bride
    getting down
    from her bed.
Her companions
    remain
    upon it.
The red veil.

Photograph, *circa* 1950s

This could be an innocuous
photograph. If you did not know.
A snap from a family album,
perhaps, a young woman politely
visiting her grandmother.
But the older woman was famous
beyond the small circle of poetry.
Her fame like a church steeple,
viewing the world's oddities
with wit from a moral stance.
She is seated on a low couch.
From her porridge bowl face,
she gazes with kindly sincerity
at the visiting young woman,
a composition of angles
seated in the upright chair
closer to the foreground.
The younger woman, her hair
crimped in wave of fashion,
wears a beaded necklace, carries
a small purse, a magazine
illustration of correctness.
Her fingers are tightly interlaced,
hooked together in a tense web.

In time, she will also become
a well-known poet and, still young,
kill herself. That is not in
the photograph. What is there
is a lamp positioned between them.
In reality, not the flattened planes
of this black and white photograph,
this ordinary lamp sits on a table
positioned just behind them.
In the photograph, its light
illuminates the older woman's
upright face and unwavering gaze.
The young woman's head seems
too close to the lamp itself.

Three Continents But the Same Moon

Hurrying home from a gallery opening
10th Street tunnel of cold wind
feeling the city a cage
but the snow glittered
under its Manhattan grime
with the moon just past full
joined in the night sky
with the spire of Grace Church.

Woken in the night but gently
by Spanish moonlight
like water flooding
in the window and outside
touching the grape vines
looking like white bones
regulator of tides and blood
companion in nights so quiet
I could hear olives dropping.

Returning to Chania by battered bus
from Iraklion and Knossos
ancient moonlight illuminates
harbor water bouzouki music zig-zag streets
and this old house on Minoan foundations
where a year has gone by late night moon
writing harbor music bouzoukia street
zig-zag water words.

Chania, Crete

After El Salvador

for Marilyn and Fernando

In bed, in sleep, in dreams
the spider of memory
    spins webs of receding time
    to the beat of a Latin rhythm.

El Salvador nightmares
rerun their familiar images.

    Friends abruptly disappear,
    neighborhood electricity
    dims from nearby torture,
    gun shots on quiet streets,
    night fires exploding hiss,
    edgy questions without answers.

No one can be trusted.

Waking now in another country,
    El Salvador nightmares
    suspended in the dark
like flies spun into cocoons.

Instead Of

Sitting on the kitchen floor
playing pots and pans with Benjamin
in this sixth floor New York
walk-up in the East Village
I overhear you talking
on the telephone to an old acquaintance
saying that you had planned
to take a freighter trip
with Miranda but instead
she went insane
and you had a baby

Flowering Tree

Fruitlessly scented mock-
orange in fresh blossom
like a frigid nymphomaniac
in white lingerie.
Or is it once again
only another of nature's
enigmatic gestures?

Night Dreaming Day

These images you know do not exist
but are more real because elliptical,
images in dreams
picture reality with a fierceness
we could not bear in waking.
They shave the beard
to show the woman's face
we once loved who became a nun
or the bird's hairy nest
to show the starving animal
rising from between two eggs,
connect the sleeping form
next to us in our bed
with the foreign landscape
we once loved and left,
pull women from underwater
to rescue the balance of our lives
but with the same saving hand
destroy the statue of two men
wrestling naked which was a present
from our closest friend.
In the freak tent of our dreams
no sight is too grotesque.
Familiar as our morning mirror
dreams connect with mathematical perfection
the masquerade of simple patterns
to become the terrifying news
whispered in the ear of day.

| | | |

In My Mother's Studio

What clearer, pure vision than childhood's?
Lifetimes spent attempting to recapture,
easily encompassing the grotesque
and the beautiful with equal clarity.
How we see is what we see.
In my mother's studio again, but now
as eldest son on short holiday.
Always working, relearning work is play.
Familiar surroundings: carefully kept brushes,
palette a summer garden mirrored
in fields, flowers, occasional building,
both in view and in paintings;
some portraits in progress,
shapes sketched in suggestion of face
or flower, freshly gessoed panels waiting,
spent tubes of paint and new ones;
space only for painting and paint,
thermos of tea, vase of pink and white
flowers, white bowl of golden fruit,
walls are color charts, photographs
of family, friends, flowers, nudes.
I struggle in my afternoon's light
with color, shapes, form. Same struggle
on rainy mornings when I was seven.
Same studio, same vision, only lacking
then technique with decades spent
relearning to say the same pure vision
that how we see is what we see.

Architect

for Hiroo Imai

River   forest path
   long view
   becomes
   hallway

Open field   place
   green hedges
   becomes
   hidden space

Light   oblique light
   like wind
   becomes
   direction

Quiet sky   stones
   memory
   becomes
   architecture

"Beauty Queen"

an assemblage by Bruce Brodie

She circles around and around
    colored lights behind her,
obscured by an almost
    opaque screen.

That familiar form precise
    when she nears the screen;
otherwise, enticing shadows:
    as in art, viewer as voyeur.

But this beauty is a tiny airplane,
    a boy's own toy,
phallus with wings
    circling within a box frame.

Symbol of a symbol:
    that cute phenomenon
of why men name their war planes
    using women's names.

Poor "Beauty Queen"
    helpless symbol
trapped in her endless circle,
    labeled with a borrowed name.

Hanging Ann Page's "Pick Up Styx"

Center piece by placing yellow template at eye level
where 'X' is indicated.

> 'X' marking place. Treasure map, road guide,
> instructions for final destination. That
> place where direction ends.

Drive nails about 1/8 to 1/4˝ deep into the wall
in 1, 2 & 3 positions.

> Anchors hold a ship in a temporary condition.
> At Madeira, we went in on small boats from
> deep water to shallow to port.

Remove yellow template and nails.

> Positions are noted. All journeys are
> motions forward in time. Although unexpected
> weather sometimes intervenes.

Put nails through corresponding loops on piece and
in the order stated hammer them into the wall.

> The course is fixed. The ship sails away.

Cup the bottom of the piece so that a cone forms
in order to get the third loop in position.

Like drying leaves curl and decay, nothing is
permanent. Not leaves, not paper, not trajectory.

Pull black string to the front of the piece.

Hanging at the still point in trajectory's arc,
time within space is sensed.

Translucent flaps should have a downward direction.

The river is reached by land or tributaries
racing downward on the map to 'X.' You may
pick up the River Styx at any point. The
boatman is patient.

Final note. Installation should be done as per
instructions provided.

Harbor, dock, boat, water.

All other impressions have been destroyed. The stones
have been defaced.

Bones

for Sylvia Glass

A book, of sorts of bones.
The artist's book handmade
utilizing nature's bones,
reminder of our own mortality.
Telling how nature takes back
into itself that which remains,
transforms from working parts
objects of contemplation.

Pages like a leather lining
previously worn next to moving flesh,
the shifting movement of skin
creating a silky, mottled patina.

Small flaps conceal bone fragments.
I know these particular bones
discovered under glass cases
in a Chinatown herbal shop.
Yet, others, desiccated by
desert days of bleaching sun,
are these forensic evidence?
Across encaustic surfaces,
smudged fingerprints—
mute, enigmatic witness
of suspicious circumstances?

But this book is a narrative
about time passing,
the not sinister voice of nature
from whom messages are
received all the time.

Archeology dovetails with history
while nature quietly
covers our receding tracks.
Bones, a half-remembered
alphabet of the body,
say that something once existed.

Stuart Appalled on Melrose Avenue

In a city where anonymity
would seem a plausible disguise,
he is never lost. In Los Angeles,
his past is always present.
Curiously, this most secretive
of Scorpios is always being identified.
For example: at a new gallery,
white rooms within white rooms,
while the elegant Japanese owner
(or perhaps tall Balinese)
makes small, perfect gestures
in casual conversation balanced
with the theatrical strokes of
the born artist Stuart, who today
is merely viewer, the secretary
(plump, beaded and forty)
suddenly and loudly exclaims,
"Stuart Allingham! Do you remember?
We were in elementary school together.
In third grade, we all thought you witty!"
The viewing viewer viewed.
He flees from further identification
down the white staircase from
the white rooms within white rooms,
the tall, elegant Japanese/Balinese owner,
his secretary with a phenomenal memory,
and Stuart stands appalled on Melrose Avenue.
A block away, the Hollywood Cemetery,
where all those other famous names
are not quite forgotten
but merely discreetly buried.

Family History

Why puzzle
    such differences
  angles of vision

partial answers
      exist
  like mismatched facts

I tell you
    family stories
  for instance

my father's mother
    climbing trees
  at seventy in her orchard

you show me
    your grandmother's
  tiny silk slippers

for feet
    created by
  footbinder's visits

Rattlesnake

Early Sunday morning ritual:
    we walk the dog
    in Griffith Park.
Semi-wilderness, green paradise,
    escape from city life.
We walk, she runs.
    Like a puppy again:
    excited, curious.

Today she freezes in mid-run.
    A rattlesnake,
    still uncoiled.
Like an alphabet character
    in a foreign language.
We step back. Danger,
    when it was
    least expected.

Survivor's Tale

Surviving a cancer
    which usually kills
is a screwdriver
the way it tightens
  the loose parts
  of one's life.

Ordinary events
  bloom again
in the clean oxygen
of newly wet dirt.
  A garden
  not a grave.

Crawling like
    a wounded animal
through despair's tunnel
and surviving into landscape,
  life is as dense
  as egg yolks.

Harsh, unexpected intimacy
   with my own death,
   not visitor this time
but patient in the cancer ward.

A hospice ending squatted
in the mind's darkest corner
   like a rat gnawing
   in a cabinet.
Frightened thoughts predicted
by other's lives.   Or deaths.

Peculiar weeks of recovery
drifting in another time zone.
   Mine a deadly form
   of deadly melanoma,
   so advanced statistics
   become my enemies.
A skin graft on my back
avoided unless by accident,
brief and shocking mirror view.

Followed by tests for which
I cannot study, cram nor crib.
   Blood scanned, bone
   scanned, brain scanned.
   Prone on a stretcher
   remote controlled
   through barium X-rays.
Doctors and nurses handling
my body as intimately as a lover.

Still among the living
   not the dead
this malignant catastrophe
prompts the inevitable question:

Is the cancer still there,
floating about
like a microscopic shark
in the aquarium of my body?

My existence not running down
to zero in the short run,
I travel through my days,
these weeks, this month,
as if nothing could go wrong,
delight in simple pleasures.

Yet beneath this placid surface
(calming my companion,
relieving friends with laughter,
understating to my family)
exists the constant question:

"Are you still there? Will you
return for a deadly visit?"

Hoping only for flat echo as answer.

I have my bulwarks against entropy.

Or, perhaps, these are normal
actions of a long and happy life,
doing those things I have
always done, will continue doing.

Planting nasturtium seeds today
expecting to live and see
their flowering in another season
and planning (that ordinary word
with incantory impact) simple
things, all in the future.

My good bulwarks—be true.

Green Hope

You give me green hope.
I fear I will die
before the year is over.
Cancer is the specter
crouched in the corner.
You say, "Next year we
will attend the dragon parade
for Chinese New Year."
Half-sick with medications,
I believe you,
not the specter.

Untitled

How living scrapes us down
to plain facts, bone truths.
Like a glacier rasping
landscape to stone.
Nothing left except pure vista.
So bare the slightest rock
seems a sign of direction.

Changes

for E.L.

The New Year's Ikebana
dries outdoors
for burning

Green pine, red berries,
bamboo like white bones.

The new year
moves forward
into a fresh arrangement.

Photo by John Rose

MICHAEL J. LAURENCE WAS BORN IN 1938 IN MINNESOTA.

Before school age it was discovered that Michael could see objects and people only as large fuzzy shapes. He was declared legally blind and upon receiving a set of glasses he ran from window to window mentally drawing large red lines around everything so that whatever happened to his sight he would never forget exactly how things looked.

He was graduated from the University of Minnesota. After two years of military service he moved to New York City and fell in love with the cinema; Godard, Fellini, and Truffaut influenced his narrative style as well as literary idols Lawrence Durrell and Virginia Woolf.

After a brief marriage and separation Michael sailed for Spain in the early 1970's living at El Robine in the coastal village of Alicante. He worked as a script writer and part-time actor for Tartar Productions. Later he would move to Chania, Crete and establish residence in the famous 16th century Villa One Angel Street where he wrote *Crete: A Travel Book* for Editions Berlitz.

After settling in Los Angeles in the late 1970's his poetry and short fiction were regularly featured in journals including *S.H.Y. Literary*

Quarterly, Athenian, Wordworks, Caterpillar, Telephone, Dreamworks and *Mudfish*. He reviewed art exhibitions in Los Angeles which were read throughout the 1980's and 90's in *Art in America, New Art Examiner, Artscribe International, Sculpture, Flash Art, Visions and Artweek*.

During this time he began a work which would eventually evolve into into a trilogy of novels reflecting his life as an expatriate in the Mediterranean.

Michael was also an artist and his art reflected his life in books. The significance of the Word, the book (as object), and references to artistic and literary figures abound. Collections of his work are found in London, Madrid, New York, Los Angeles, and Athens.

Stuart Allingham

in the mire of time,
You slowly gnaw my life away.
Apollinaire 'The Mouse'

We knew that we had damned ourselves
Dbd The Odyssey

Rain clouds over New Mexico mountains —
layers of slate grey white at the top.
over distant blue mountains.
Light falls in rain streaked shafts.
Time moves slowly as the train
across this landscape and stopped
and ringed about with mountains.
You never liked being surrounded
by mountains or even a distant view.
Now your life is circled
by time closing in.
this train, this familiar landscape,
my lifetime of memories
this train carrying me to our final visit,
this familiar landscape once again,
my lifetime of memories
begun with your first gift of life itself.
Rain draws near. The light fades.

6/4/89

Rain draws nearer across this empty landscape,
the light slowly fades
the view changes as the light slowly fades.

Ordinary events
bloom again.
into explorations of memory
All else, fading
stars half
of night time roads.
Night profile fading silver
silver tracks
made tense.
Night tracks fading silver
tracks mark
time passing.
simple things flower
with the impact
of vision.

as a garden
rising from scoured dirt
a garden not a grave
in the newly wet dirt,
a garden
not a grave.

Ordinary events
bloom again
in the newly wet dirt.
A garden
not a grave.

Ordinary events
bloom again
in the newly wet dirt.
A garden
not a grave.